Unit 1

Take a New Step

Contents

I Can

I can  the .
mix   eggs

I can  the  .

mix   eggs

3

I can  the .
mix   milk

I can  the .
mix   milk

Kitten can mop the milk.

Can I?

I can  the 🍅.
wash   tomato

 can  the  .

Mom   mop   mud

9

Can I  the  ?
mix   salad

10

Can I  the ?
     drink   milk

I can  the 🍚 .
eat   salad

I Am

I can  .

jump

I am .
sad

Can I ?
jump

We can  .

jump

I am  !
happy

We Can

I can 🐱 the 🐱 .
pat   cat

The  can .
cat   eat

21

The  can  .
    cat   nap

We can .

nap

23

I am  .
happy

Sam Can See

Sam can see the .
bench

Sam can see the  .
pond

Sam can see the  .

ducks

Sam can see the  .

bird

Sam can see .

Mom

We can see the  Sam.
waves

Sam can see the ☀ .

sun

We can  Sam.

sit

34

Sam can see the  .

sand

We can  Sam.
dig

I Can

DECODABLE WORDS	HIGH-FREQUENCY WORDS
Target Phonics Elements	the
Initial and Final Consonant *m*	**Review:** can, I

Can I?

DECODABLE WORDS	HIGH-FREQUENCY WORDS
Target Phonics Elements	the
Initial and Final Consonant *m*	**Review:** can, I

I Am

DECODABLE WORDS	HIGH-FREQUENCY WORDS
Target Phonics Elements	we
Short *a*: am	**Review:** can, I

We Can

DECODABLE WORDS	HIGH-FREQUENCY WORDS
Target Phonics Elements	we
Short *a*: am	**Review:** can, I, the

Sam Can See

DECODABLE WORDS	HIGH-FREQUENCY WORDS
Target Phonics Elements	see
Initial *s*: Sam	**Review:** can, the

Sam

DECODABLE WORDS	HIGH-FREQUENCY WORDS
Target Phonics Elements	see
Initial *s*: Sam	**Review:** can, the, we

HIGH-FREQUENCY WORDS TAUGHT TO DATE
Grade K
can
I
see
the
we

DECODING SKILLS TAUGHT TO DATE
Initial and final consonant *m*; short *a*; initial *s*